How To

BE A GENIUS

BE A GENIUS

By JONATHAN HANCOCK

Illustrated by
Alan Rowe

FRANKLIN WATTS
A Division of Scholastic Inc.
New York   Toronto   London   Auckland   Sydney
Mexico City   New Delhi   Hong Kong
Danbury, Connecticut

For Phoebe, Alice, and Maddie

First published 2000 by Oxford University Press
Great Clarendon Street, Oxford OX2 6DP

First American edition 2001 by Franklin Watts
A Division of Scholastic Inc.
90 Sherman Turnpike
Danbury, CT 06816

2009 2008 2007 2006
10 9 8 7 6 5 4 3 2

Catalog details are available from the Library of Congress
Cataloging-in-Publication Data

ISBN-13: 978-0-531-14648-4 (lib. bdg.)
ISBN-10: 0-531-14648-0 (lib. bdg.)
ISBN-13: 978-0-531-13996-7 (pbk.)
ISBN-10: 0-531-13996-4 (pbk.)

Printed in China

Contents

BECOMING A GENIUS

Anyone can make discoveries and come up with revolutionary inventions. It doesn't matter what school you go to, which subjects you're good at, how much money you've got, or how old you are. As long as you use your brain effectively, you can achieve amazing things.

In this book you'll meet geniuses from many walks of life. You'll get to know scientists like Charles Darwin and Albert Einstein, who came up with incredible new ideas that changed the way people saw the world and the universe forever.

You'll meet inventors like Thomas Edison, who thought up something new every ten days or so. And you'll look over the shoulder of the multitalented artist, inventor, and engineer Leonardo da Vinci to see how he got things done.

All these geniuses were unique individuals, but if you look carefully you'll find out that they did have things in common. In this book you will get to see how you measure up, and find out how to maximize your chances of becoming a great genius.

In this book you will

- test every area of your brainpower

- predict how likely you are to become a famous genius

- find out how to think up brilliant ideas

- learn about intelligence tests and discover how to make high scores

- investigate the way computers think

- find out what makes someone a genius and learn how you can become one, too

The secret ways that you can learn to think like a genius are revealed in this book—so get ready to boost your brainpower to brilliance!

CHAPTER ONE

WHAT IS A GENIUS?

$E = mc^2$. That's the part most people know of Einstein's theories of relativity. It looks like a simple enough equation, but in fact the theories behind it are extremely complicated.

Einstein's discovery changed the way scientists saw time and space. Our understanding of the universe changed forever—and all thanks to a man who failed his school exams, never wore socks, and once even forgot where he lived!

Now is it 42, or 24?

Albert Einstein fits the image many people have of a genius. Not only did he achieve incredible things in physics, he also *looked* like a genius, with his odd clothes and wild white hair. In one famous photograph, he's sticking his tongue out at the camera, and there's a mischievous glint in his eye.

Einstein was an unusual character, and he had unusual thoughts—so unusual that he was able to make revolutionary discoveries. He was a genius because he achieved an entirely new level of thought.

You don't have to be a scientist to be a genius. Here are a few more examples of genius at work.

See the Mona Lisa's smile, and you know immediately that Leonardo da Vinci painted with genius. No one else could have achieved that magic. Da Vinci took art to new levels, and even today his work opens our eyes to new discoveries about the world.

To lovers of classical music, Wolfgang Amadeus Mozart was unquestionably a genius. He did things with sound that no one else could do. His music continues to touch people's emotions in a unique way. Scientists have even discovered that listening to Mozart boosts your brainpower, which shows that his genius is passed on through his work.

World Chess Champion Gary Kasparov uses his genius to take on the most powerful computers, often out-thinking them in ways that even the latest programs can't grasp.

Trevor Baylis invented a clockwork radio that revolutionized the lives of millions of people. His invention was itself a revolution, treating a common piece of equipment in an entirely new way. It seems like a simple idea, but without the genius of this one special man, perhaps no one would ever have invented it.

To be a genius, you have to be more than just good at what you do. You have to do it in a new and different way. You must do more than teach or entertain or help other people. A true genius changes people's lives by showing them that more than they have ever dreamed of is possible.

10

It's not surprising that geniuses are often very quirky people. Perhaps they have to be a little different to come up with their unusually brilliant ideas. This book is about the men and women who have advanced our understanding of the world and our knowledge of what is possible.

You look odd enough to be a genius! Come in!

If you have a brain, you can be a genius—you just have to learn to *think* like one. The geniuses in this book emerged in different times, from a wide range of countries and backgrounds. They could have been ordinary, but they used their brains in extraordinary ways to become famous and to achieve great things.

Follow these four simple but powerful rules and you, too, can become a genius:

- start thinking creatively
- improve your memory
- boost your senses and coordination
- seize new opportunities for learning

You also need to develop some important qualities of genius, common to many of the great names featured in this book. You must have

 unlimited interest in your chosen subjects and pursuits

the persistence to succeed, despite any obstacle

an ability to work with others

the bravery to challenge even the experts, and to go farther than anyone has gone before

The secrets of genius have fascinated us since ancient times. Various systems have been designed to measure brainpower and to identify potential geniuses. You're going to learn how to give your best performance in every kind of test.

CHAPTER TWO

TEST YOUR GENIUS

At the end of the book, the Genius Challenge will measure how close you are to being a genius. But first take a test to find out how strong your brain is now. Allow yourself no more than 20 minutes to do the test, then turn to page 19 to check the answers and find your current Genius Grade.

Become a Genius
GENIUS TEST

WHAT YOU'LL NEED
* a pen
* paper
* a brain (preferably your own)

WHAT TO DO
Answer these questions and record your answers.

1. Observation
Can you spot the detail missing from each of these pictures?

a)   b)

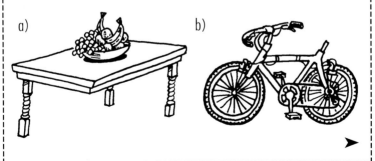

➤

c)

d)

2. Words

a) Which word doesn't fit?

cup, saucer, plate, kitchen, bowl

b) Which of the following words is the opposite of "quiet"?

silent, very, noisy, still, fast

c) Add one letter to make a familiar word:

T H I _ K I N G

d) Which two words from the following list have the same meaning?

clever, honest, happy, trustworthy, beautiful

3. Numbers

a) Which of the following numbers is different from the rest?

7, 3, 10, 5, 9

b) Which of these number pairs is different from the rest?

6 3   8 1   2 7   4 8   9 0

➤

c) If 692 turns into 926, what does 715 turn into?

$$571, 517, 157, 175$$

d) What's the next number in the following sequence?

12 10 8 6 _

4. Shapes

a) Which shape comes next in the following sequence?

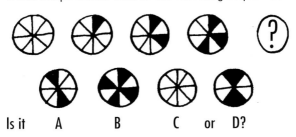

Is it   A   B   C   or   D?

b) If 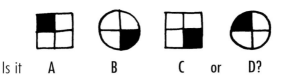 turns into ,

what does turn into?

Is it   A   B   C   or   D?

c) Which of the following shapes doesn't fit with the rest?

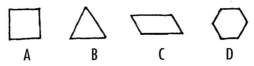

A   B   C   D

➤

15

d) Which one of the jigsaw pieces will fit the puzzle?

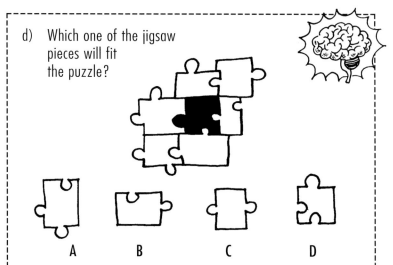

A   B   C   D

5. Memory

Read through the following fifteen words for no more than one minute, then cover the page and see how many you can write down from memory, in any order:

hat, pen, clock, light, wall, book, blue, hole, short, mouse, heat, well, time, nail, line

6. Logic

Oliver is older than Daisy and Alice. Alice is older than Daisy. Oliver's brother is named Jim. Alice has an older sister. Daisy has no sisters.

From that information, which of the following statements is definitely true? (There can be more than one answer.)

a) Daisy is younger than Alice
b) Oliver is older than Jim
c) Daisy is an only child
d) Daisy and Alice are friends
e) Daisy and Alice are both younger than Oliver
f) Alice could have a brother

➤

7. Creativity

What could the following drawing represent?
Write down as many different possibilities as you
can think of.

8. Senses

Give yourself an honest score, between 0 and 10 points, for
each of the following questions:

a) How varied is the music you listen to (from 0 for no music
   at all, to 10 for a completely varied musical collection)?
b) How much can you rely on your sense of smell?
c) How much enjoyment do you get from tasting different
   flavors?
d) How good is your eyesight?
e) How often do you do things that rely on delicate touch and
   a steady hand?
f) How much do you enjoy traveling to new places with a
   variety of sights, sounds, tastes, and smells?
g) How much interest do you have in birds, animals, plants,
   weather, and the countryside?

9. Physical Health

Answer either "never," "sometimes," or "regularly" to each
question. How often do you:

a) raise your heart rate for more than 20 minutes
   (e.g., by swimming, running, cycling, fast-walking)?
b) dance?
c) play precision sports, such as archery, darts, golf, or bowling?
d) practice flexibility and stretching?
e) work on your strength (e.g., lifting weights, doing push-
   ups)?

➤

f) practice your balance (e.g., gymnastics, tai chi, yoga)?

g) work on your hand-eye coordination (e.g., juggling, computer games)?

10. Interests

a) Write down all the subjects that you find interesting at school.

b) Write down all things you do outside school that you find interesting.

c) Write down anything else that you would like to do or find out about, but that you haven't gotten around to yet.

11. Teamwork

How many different people (e.g., teacher, parent, sister, friend, uncle, neighbor) would you ask for help with

a) your homework?

b) your hobbies?

c) ideas you have?

12. Persistence

Answer the following questions with either "yes" or "no":

a) Do you have any hobbies that you've enjoyed for more than a year?

b) Have any of your friendships lasted for more than three years?

c) If you have difficulty with your schoolwork, do you keep trying until you find a solution?

d) Have you ever taken part in a sponsored event (e.g., a race) and completed the challenge?

e) Do you regularly get to the end of books?

Answers

For parts 1–4, give yourself 5 points for each correct answer.
1. a) table leg b) bicycle seat c) reflection of hairbrush d) letter K
2. a) kitchen b) noisy c) N d) honest, trustworthy
3. a) 151 b) 10 c) 48 d) 4
4. a) B b) D c) D d) D
5. You get 2 points for every word you remembered.
6. The answers are a, e, and f. Award yourself 2 points for each one you got right.
7. Give yourself 1 point for every idea you wrote down.
8. You already have your scores.
9. You get 0 for "never," 1 point for "sometimes," and 2 points for "regularly."
10. and 11. You get 1 point for every person or interest listed.
12. Award yourself nothing for "no" and 2 points for "yes."

Find your genius grade

0–100 points: Genius Grade 1—needs work

101–150 points: Genius Grade 2—below average

151–200 points: Genius Grade 3—average

201–250 points: Genius Grade 4—good

251–300 points: Genius Grade 5—very good

301–350 points: Genius Grade 6—excellent

351 points or more: Genius Grade 7—outstanding; true genius material

CHAPTER THREE

BEGINNINGS OF GENIUS

Anyone can become a genius, but for some the journey to greatness is more of a struggle than it is for others. It certainly helps if you have a supportive family, help from a company or organization, an inspiring place to live, and a supportive community. But these benefits are by no means essential. As you'll see, a difficult upbringing sometimes helps! It can be just what someone needs to make them determined to succeed against all odds.

Genius in the Genes? ....

No, not *that* kind of genes!

Some geniuses seem to have been born to greatness as members of very smart and illustrious families. This doesn't guarantee future success, but it provides a very helpful starting point.

Genius Families
Part I: Sicily, third century B.C.

Archimedes was born into one of the most famous families in Sicily in 287 B.C. Some people say he was related to the ruler Hiero. Archimedes's father, Pheidias, was an astronomer who was already thinking great thoughts, trying to figure out the dimensions of the universe. This sparked Archimedes's imagination, and he set out on a long career of exploration, trying to answer some big questions of his own about math and science. His many important discoveries paved the way for all the physicists and mechanics who came after him.

That's Dad, measuring the universe again!

Genius Families

Part II: Germany, eighteenth century

Johann Sebastian Bach was born into a musical family, but he still had to struggle for his success. His older brother, Johann Christian, was a skillful organist who taught him to play at an early age. But for some reason, J.C. refused to share his collection of books. So the young J.S. used to sneak in at night and copy the music books he wanted by the light of the moon. Even though he was a renowned singer, violinist, organist, and composer by the age of nineteen, Bach still did everything he could to improve. It's said that he once traveled on foot more than 250 miles (400 kilometers) to see a famous organist perform.

Bach became one of the greatest classical composers of all time. His family background was helpful, but he was also one of the hardest-working composers in history. At the height of his career he was playing for church services, heading up a school, writing music to order, and composing and rehearsing a complicated piece of music for his choir every single week.

Let's see... choir rehearsal, church service, write organ composition, school staff meeting—a quiet day today.

Genius Organizations ....

Many great thinkers and creators find it helpful to join groups of like-minded people. Often they work hard to get into the most supportive and inspiring organizations and societies.

Choose Your Friends
Part I: Egypt, third century B.C.

Archimedes moved from Sicily to Egypt to study at the mathematical school in Alexandria. There he made friends with many local scientists. He enjoyed creating puzzles for his fellow students and taking part in thinking games.

What do you think of this? I got it from my friend Rubik.

The great Italian painter and inventor Leonardo da Vinci was lucky enough to be taught by a master artist named Verrocchio. Verrocchio was able to put da Vinci in touch with many of the most talented local people, and later he joined the Company of Saint Luke, a guild of scientists and artists.

Choose Your Friends
Part II: Oxford, England, around 1650

Christopher Wren is one of the most famous architects in history. He designed St. Paul's Cathedral in London, as well as hundreds of other amazing structures.

Also a great scientist, astronomer, and mathematician, Wren spent his life working his way into the country's most prestigious organizations.

After leaving school at age fourteen and working at several jobs, Wren made it to Oxford University in his mid-teens. At Oxford he met many brilliant thinkers. Some of them later helped him establish the Royal Society, an organization designed to encourage great discoveries. His colleagues there included Isaac Newton, the genius who made important discoveries about light, math and, most notably, gravity.

Genius Places ....

Some cities and countries have proved to be great places for encouraging geniuses. Archimedes, for example, studied in the great library in Alexandria, and Leonardo da Vinci gained greatly from his time in the inspirational cities of Florence and Milan. Florence was a particularly good place for any would-be genius to hang out. It was at the center of many regions and welcomed travelers from all over. It maintained a healthy rivalry with nearby cities such as Venice and Rome. And there were plenty of other intelligent, ambitious people there for da Vinci to learn from.

Albert Einstein had two favorite places to work: Oxford, England, and Princeton, New Jersey. He said he liked the architecture and the light, and found both places to be quiet, friendly university towns where he could work happily and productively.

Genius Times ....

Some periods in history have been especially good for
aspiring geniuses. If your particular genius leads you
to build a time machine one day, you might want to
set the controls for some of these special destinations.

The Right Place, the Right Time
Part I: Greece, fifth century B.C.

This was a prosperous age, very rich in geniuses. Visit here and
you'll meet Aeschylus, Sophocles, and Euripides, great
playwrights at a time when poetry and drama were treated as
sporting events. These geniuses had
amazing records of success
in the fiercely fought
competitions.

And in the red corner...

All these men were famous philosophers, too. They used their
understanding of human behavior to write thrilling, bloody,
terrifying plays that are still performed today. You'll also meet
Socrates, the philosopher who asked the biggest question of all:
how do we really know what's true and what isn't? He made
people question all their old beliefs and changed the world by
inventing logical thinking.

The Right Place, the Right Time

Part II: Italy, fifteenth century

Hundreds of thousands of people had been killed off by the Black Death, the terrible plague that swept through Europe in the fourteenth century. Afterward all the riches were shared among far fewer people, so there were more opportunities for geniuses to advance themselves. This was a time when art, philosophy, and invention all flourished. We call it the Renaissance, which means "rebirth."

One of the most important figures of the Renaissance in Italy was Michelangelo. He became the most famous sculptor in history, and was also an ingenious painter and architect. He spent four years in Rome painting the ceiling of the Sistine Chapel, one of the most ambitious and impressive works of art ever completed.

Other geniuses of the Italian Renaissance were painters Raphael and Titian, political writer and thinker Machiavelli, and one of the greatest geniuses of all time, Leonardo da Vinci, who was a painter, inventor, engineer, botanist, weather forecaster, and musician. There was excitement in the air, the buzz of new discoveries, ideas, and possibilities. And there were plenty of wealthy people around to buy their paintings. Da Vinci was born at the right time in a place perfectly suited to encouraging his awesome genius.

The Right Place, the Right Time

Part III: England, sixteenth century

The geniuses of this period owe a great debt of thanks to their ruler, the much-loved Queen Elizabeth I. She believed she had to be an inspiration to the nation, and made sure that pictures of herself were distributed far and wide. She gathered at court the greatest minds, chose her advisors carefully, and led England through many perilous years. Her brilliance as a ruler allowed many geniuses to flourish, such as philosopher Francis Bacon and the most famous writer of all time, William Shakespeare. Shakespeare made the most of the age he was born into, with its explosion of knowledge, foreign influences, and new ideas. He wrote the best-loved plays in history and changed theater forever.

Go, I command you! And do not return until you have created at least three works of genius.

How likely are you to follow in the footsteps of Socrates, Michelangelo, and Shakespeare? Complete the following questionnaire to check your advantages as an aspiring genius.

Become a Genius
CHECK YOUR BACKGROUND

WHAT YOU'LL NEED
* ✱ a pen
* ✱ paper

WHAT TO DO
Answer the following questions:

1. Families
Do you have...

a relative who went to a college or university, who can give you advice on your future career?

a family tradition of a particular kind of work, or a family business, to get you started?

grandparents to talk to, for their wisdom and experience?

family vacations or days off, so that you can learn from new people and places?

2. Organizations
Are you a member of...

a school or college, to get help from teachers and friends?

any after-school classes, for extra inspiration?

a library, to help you build your knowledge?

a club or society, for specific learning and training?

3. Places
Do you have...

a college or university nearby, to provide an atmosphere of learning?

➤

a museum nearby, to provide information?

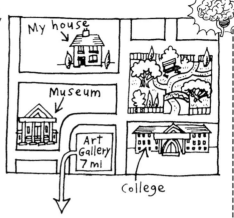

an art gallery nearby, for inspiration?

countryside or a park nearby, for quiet thought?

4. Time Period

In this day and age, do you think that...

anyone can be successful, as long as they try hard enough?

everyone can try foods, books, music, and films from around the world?

we can all find access to the Internet—at home, in school, or by visiting a library?

telephones, faxes, and e-mail are easy to use and available everywhere?

Check your success...

Give yourself one point every time you answered "yes" to a question.

0–4 points: It's going to be a struggle for you to become a genius, but it is still possible. Bach was committed enough to overcome his difficulties. Da Vinci was born to a peasant girl in a small town, but he still rose to greatness—and so can you.

5–8 points: You have an average chance of achieving the rank of genius. There are probably more opportunities for boosting your brainpower than you think, so keep your eyes open every day.

9–12 points: You stand a better chance than most of making it to the top. Don't be afraid to go that little bit farther in your quest for genius. You need to stay focused on your goals.

13–16 points: You have the perfect background for becoming a genius—and you should make the most of it. Many other hopefuls have shown early promise, then fallen by the wayside. Keep up your enthusiasm and determination, and make use of everything and everyone you've got!

CHAPTER FOUR

DISCOVERIES AND INVENTIONS

It only takes one moment of genius to change the world, as long as you're brave enough to take a few risks.

Four rules of invention, plus another four, makes... seven?

You, too, can change the world with your genius. Just study the Eight Secrets of Invention and you will be well on your way.

1. Delight in Your Chosen Subjects ....

Most of the geniuses in this book were completely obsessed with their subject. Some wanted to find the answers to questions, or solve problems, that had puzzled people for years, sometimes centuries. Others pursued new ideas or creative visions that only they could see.

The Patient Clockmaker

England, eighteenth century

John Harrison solved the "longitude problem," one of the great puzzles of his time. He invented a clock that could measure time at sea (where pendulum clocks are useless), and that made it possible for sailors to accurately calculate their position east or west (their longitude) for the first time. It was a problem that had baffled many great thinkers, and Harrison pursued a solution with incredible determination. This was only possible because of his love of invention and experimentation.

When he was still a teenager, Harrison demonstrated this love of learning when a visiting clergyman loaned him a textbook he'd been eager to read. Instead of just leafing through it, Harrison wrote it out word for word. He copied and labeled every diagram and added his own notes.

But if you'd asked me, I have a spare copy...

Still Doing Your Homework?

England and Princeton, NJ, late twentieth century

When ten-year-old Andrew Wiles was walking home one day, he stopped into his local library. There he read a book that would change his life. In the book was one of the greatest mathematical puzzles of all time, Fermat's Last Theorem. Mathematician Pierre Fermat once wrote that he had discovered the answer to a tricky problem, but he never wrote it down— and nobody since had been able to offer a solution. Wiles was so intrigued by the idea that he decided to crack the puzzle himself. He loved math riddles, and his delight in the subject gave him all the energy he needed to get going on his quest.

Thirty-four years later, on June 27, 1997, while working as a professor at Princeton University, Wiles won a prize of $50,000 for solving the conundrum that had baffled the world for more than 350 years. His interest had kept him going, and his delight in math only grew stronger with each setback.

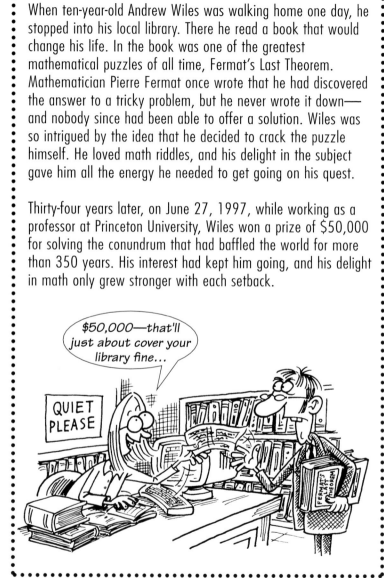

$50,000—that'll just about cover your library fine...

2. Learn from Past Geniuses ....

Geniuses think new thoughts and dream up original ideas, but they need to start with information already available. They must be able to learn from their predecessors.

In ancient Greece, each great thinker learned from the last. Socrates taught Plato, the "grandfather of philosophy," who taught Aristotle, the inventor of logical reasoning, who in turn taught Alexander the Great, perhaps the most powerful ruler in history.

In his early twenties, Albert Einstein sent out letter after letter asking famous scientists to take him on as an assistant so that he could learn from them. Not one of them replied. Instead he had to read as many of their books as he could get hold of.

When Einstein's career later took off, he made use of the discoveries of two geniuses from the past, Isaac Newton and James Clerk Maxwell. These men had very different theories about time and space, but Einstein took a fresh look at them and came up with a new way of looking at the universe: his General Theory of Relativity, with its centerpiece, $E = mc^2$.

Pay great attention to the work others have done before you, because only then will you be able to take it a step further.

3. Learn Your Subject Matter Thoroughly

Once you've decided on the areas that interest you, do everything you can to learn all there is to know about them. Don't restrict yourself: read and learn as widely as possible. Here are just some of the varied subjects great geniuses have studied.

William Shakespeare: history, languages, law, literature, math, music, politics, psychology, science, sports.

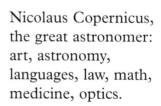

Nicolaus Copernicus, the great astronomer: art, astronomy, languages, law, math, medicine, optics.

Leonardo da Vinci: acoustics, anatomy, botany, conjuring, geology, horses, geometry, mechanics, music, painting, sculpture, weather-forecasting.

Martha Graham, American dancer and choreographer, whose brilliance changed dance forever: animals, art, history, literature, myths and legends, poetry, psychology, religion.

Geniuses are good at finding inspiration in everything they read and learn about. They are naturally inquisitive, so they build up huge stores of information on many different subjects. To be a genius in any one subject, you need to harvest information from many fields. Read widely, then focus your knowledge in the direction of your genius.

4. The Power of Cooperation...............

There are many well-known genius partnerships and groups. Great thinkers seem to be naturally drawn to other great thinkers, and together they achieve amazing things.

Francis Crick and James Watson worked together to unravel the structure of deoxyribonucleic acid (DNA), the complicated chemical that contains the biological "blueprint" for every living being. Watson got Crick interested in DNA. They bounced ideas off each other, discussed many different theories, and made a joint discovery through powerful teamwork. Together they revolutionized biology, as well as our understanding of human life.

Orville and Wilbur Wright worked together to build the first airplanes. Marie Curie formed a team with her husband, Pierre, and they made crucial discoveries about radioactivity and X rays. Even Michelangelo had a team behind him when he painted the Sistine Chapel. He's the only name people remember, but there were many other people helping him.

Find friends who are interested in the same things as you, and work with them to give even more energy to your work.

5. Create a Thinking Zone....................

Put some thought into where you do your best thinking. Geniuses often use special "thinking zones" to boost their brainpower.

The great French novelist Marcel Proust lined his study with cork to create perfect silence. British dictionary writer Samuel Johnson did his best work listening to the purring of his cat.

Perhaps you prefer listening to music while you work. If so, try Mozart. Recent research suggests that listening to Mozart's music can boost intelligence and creativity.

Some geniuses find that water helps them think. Einstein was an avid sailor. One modern-day inventor has many of his best ideas while he's in the swimming pool. A Japanese inventor named Naka Mats holds his breath and sinks underwater when he needs to do some really deep thinking. Mats also has a whole range of different-colored rooms for tackling different kinds of problems. It must work, because his inventions have made him a billionaire!

So why don't I have any good ideas?

Where you think can be an important factor in how well you think.

6. Ask the Right Questions ....

Questioning is a very important part of inventing.
Here are some of the most useful things you can ask:

 What can be added? A chemist once knocked
over a bottle of collodion, a plastic substance.
The collodion stuck some of the pieces of
broken bottle together. He realized that it could
be added to glass to make it safer. Now many
panes of glass have a plastic layer in the middle,
thanks to this chemist's clever idea.

 How else could this be used? In 1971, Bob Brown
was tinkering with an electric guitar in his
garage. He accidentally crossed two wires, and
there was a high-pitched shriek of sound that
sent a group of rats scurrying away in terror.
Bob realized that his amplifying equipment
could be put to another use, and he designed a
gadget for repelling rats. He's now a millionaire.

What can be adapted for a new use? A waffle-seller at the 1905 World's Fair spotted an ice cream stand nearby and had a brilliant idea. He molded one of his flat waffles into a cone, filled it with ice cream—and the rest is history.

 What if mistakes are lucky? When Clarence Crane's mint-making machine malfunctioned and started stamping holes in the mints, he could have thrown them all away and started again. Instead, he noticed that these new mints-with-holes were even better, and now around 30 billion packets are sold every year.

The mints are great, but I think I got a bit carried away!

 Can the same thing be done more cheaply? Antoine Feuchtwanger was selling sausages in the United States in the 1880s. Rather than giving customers at his stand plates and cutlery, he wanted to save money—and dishwashing—so he started selling the sausages inside bread rolls. And so the hot dog was born!

Geniuses are constantly asking questions. Can it be done faster, made bigger, combined with other ideas, rearranged?

Don't worry about the right answers. First make sure you're asking the right questions.

7. Be Ready for Revelation ....

When something catches your interest, it might be telling you something important.

Galileo, the Italian mathematician, physicist, and astronomer, was daydreaming in church when he spotted a chandelier swaying from side to side. Suddenly something clicked in his brain, and he knew the answer to the laws ruling how pendulums swing.

It's very important that you recognize your good ideas. Great thoughts can occur any time, any place.

Archimedes was supposedly taking a bath when he had one of his best ideas, inspired by the way the water level moved up the tub as he got in. He shouted "Eureka!" ("I've found it!"), and was so excited that he forgot he wasn't wearing any clothes and ran down the road stark naked!

I've got it! (But I kinda feel like I've forgotten something...)

8. Publicize Your Discoveries ....

In 1482, Leonardo da Vinci wrote a long letter to a nobleman in Milan, asking for a job. In the letter he described some of his inventions and ideas, including

* portable bridges
* ladders
* cannons
* tanks
* catapults
* viaducts
* sculptures

Not surprisingly, he got the job.

Once you're sure of your inventions and ideas, tell people about them. Nobody's going to know about your genius—or benefit from it—unless you make some noise.

CHAPTER FIVE

TESTING FOR GENIUS

How do you measure genius? The great men and women who appear in this book accomplished incredible things and proved their genius in many different ways. Is it possible to measure intelligence if it comes in so many different forms?

First of all, you have to decide what intelligence is. And that depends on where you live!

If you grew up in some areas of Africa or the Pacific Islands, you might have been taught that intelligence is how good you are at talking to other people and getting along with them. In these traditional cultures, fast thinking is not always best. In fact, in the Baganda tribe in Uganda, the cleverest people are thought to be those who act slowly and cautiously, making very careful decisions. The Bagandan word for intelligence is *ngware*, which means slow, careful, and straightforward.

45

On the other hand, the Western world tends to value speed of thought. We have developed tests that measure people's skill at giving answers to written questions, within a time limit.

Perhaps you've heard of IQ tests?

IQ stands for Intelligence Quotient. These tests were developed to try to measure people's brainpower. They were designed to be used by teachers to assess their students, by employers eager to find clever people to work for them, and by anyone who wants to find out how intelligent they are.

The first IQ tests were created in the early 1900s by a Frenchmen named Alfred Binet. He had noticed that most of the people getting into college were from the upper classes, and he thought this was unfair.

Binet saw the need for a system to measure intelligence that had nothing to do with how much factual information someone had been able to learn, or the educational opportunities they had had. He invented what he hoped would be a fair test of a person's brainpower.

Binet decided to see how good people were at basic word, number, and shape puzzles, and to find out how comfortable they were with language. His tests also took age into account.

IQ tests determine your mental age, which may well be different from your real age. For example, a clever ten-year-old could have a mental age of twelve. Measuring people against others of the same age produces IQ scores. The higher your score, the more intelligent you are supposed to be. The average IQ is 100.

Unfortunately, these tests can only measure certain skills, and some people think they're not very accurate. If you're shown the tricks, you can easily boost your score—so perhaps people with high IQs are just good at doing IQ tests! Binet hoped his tests would be used to chart children's progress in school, but many people today are concerned that the tests label some children as not being very smart, rather than helping them improve. Binet would not have liked that. He knew that his tests only measured a certain type of intelligence.

IQ tests are still used today, and it's useful to be good at them—but IQ isn't everything. It's important to remember that many of the geniuses in this book probably wouldn't have had very high scores. Einstein, for example, wasn't very good at math, so he might have had difficulty solving some of the puzzles.

If you have to take an IQ test, here are some tips to help you do your best. In fact, you can try these tips with whatever sort of mental challenge you're tackling.

Tip 1: Think positively

Tackle each question enthusiastically, try to enjoy the test, and don't let fear hold you back. Treat the test as a fun challenge.

Tip 2: Relax your mind

Before you start, spend a few moments with your eyes closed, breathing deeply and slowly to calm your mind. It might help to picture yourself in a nice, relaxing place. Try to imagine all the colors and sounds, and let your imagination come alive. It's important to go into any test with your mind open and working creatively. But don't get *too* relaxed!

Tip 3: Check the clock

Most IQ tests have to be completed in a certain amount of time, so you need to know how long you've got. Always make sure you know how quickly you need to work. Don't go so fast that you make silly mistakes, but don't waste time.

Tip 4: Read the questions carefully

Many people lose points simply by misreading a question. Don't assume you know what a question means right away. Read it through a couple of times to be absolutely sure.

Tip 5: Doodle

Many great geniuses, like painter Pablo Picasso, explorer Christopher Columbus, and composer Ludwig von Beethoven, used to jot down their thoughts in doodles and scribbles. Always make sure you have some scratch paper for making notes and trying out different answers. Try using colored pens or pencils to help you think creatively.

Tip 6:   Figure out what type of question it is

Most IQ tests use the same basic questions, and you can become familiar with the main types. Here are four of the most popular types of questions.

Odd one out

In these questions, you are given a group of words, numbers, or shapes, and asked to name the one that doesn't fit. This means all but one of the items have something in common. You need to determine what that thing is, so that you can spot the one item that's different.

For example:
Which is the odd one out?
>   lion, spaniel, tiger, cheetah, leopard

The answer is spaniel. Four of the animals have something in common: lion, tiger, cheetah, and leopard are all types of big cats. A spaniel, on the other hand, is a type of dog—so the spaniel must be the odd one out.

Sometimes the answer is easy to spot, but often you have to think very carefully and run through lots of possibilities in your head. Just keep asking yourself questions until inspiration hits.

Here's another example:
Which is the odd one out?

        hair, pipe, hill, bucket, comb

You might ask yourself:
"Does this have something to do with heads?" because "hair" and "comb" are on the list—but none of the other words seems to fit.

"Is there a connection with water?" because both the bucket and the pipe could carry water—but again, none of the other words ties in.

"Does it have something to do with the way the words are written?" IQ questions can be a bit tricky. In this case, you'll see that all of the words except one have the same number of letters, giving you the odd one out: "bucket."

Same/opposite

With these questions, you have to show that you know when words mean the same thing, and when words have opposite meanings. Always read these questions especially carefully.

Here's an example:
Which of the following words is the opposite of "strong"?
muscle, head, weak, empty, sad

Often there are words in the list to confuse you, such as "muscle." Your mind will tell you instantly that there is a connection between "strong" and "muscle," but is it the right connection? You're looking for the opposite of "strong," so muscle isn't the answer. It often helps to put the word in a sentence, or several different sentences. If a strong man lost his power, he would be... If the coffee wasn't very strong, you might call it... If I wasn't strong at football, I would be... Asking all these questions would lead you straight to the answer: "weak."

Here's another example:
Which of the following words means the same as "saw"?
scissors, watched, blue, kite, angry

Scissors are a bit like a saw, because they cut things. It's not exactly the same, though, so that can't be the answer. In fact, none of the words seems to be like a saw, so perhaps this is a different kind of "saw."

Try putting the word in some other sentences: "I saw my friend." "You saw him on television." As soon as you do this, you'll realize that the word "watched" will also fit in the same sentences: "I watched my friend." "You watched him on television." So "watched" must be the right answer.

This becomes that

If 2 becomes 4, then 6 becomes
10, 12, 13, or 16

The answer is 12. To solve this type of question, you must figure out how one thing becomes another. What has happened to 2 for it to become 4? Has it had 2 added to it? If so, you would have to add 2 to 6 to get the answer—but 8 isn't there in the list of possible solutions, so that can't be it.

If you double 2 it becomes 4, so perhaps you have to double 6 to find the answer. Is 12 there in the list? Yes! So 12 must be the right answer.

Sometimes these questions are written like this:
"but" is to "tub" as "pan" is to
hat, nip, top, or nap

"Is to" is just the same as "becomes." Just ask yourself: if the word "but" turns into the word "tub," what happens to it? The answer is that it is written backward, so you have to do the same thing to "pan" to come up with the solution: "nap."

Patterns and sequences
In these questions, you are given a sequence of numbers, letters, words, or shapes, and you have to decide what comes next. To solve them, you need to figure out what kind of sequence it is.

Here is an example:
What comes next in the following sequence?

a e i m q

Is it b, u, z, n, *or* r?

If you count how many letters there are between *a* and *e* in the alphabet, you'll find that it's three. There are also three letters between *e* and *i, i* and *m*, and so on. So there must be three letters between *q* and the next letter in the sequence. The answer has to be *u*.

Here's another example:
Which shape comes next?

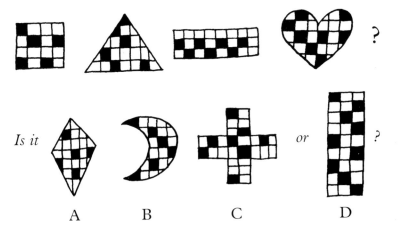

Is it   A   B   C   *or*   D   ?

How does the sequence work? If you look carefully, you'll see that each shape has one more section filled in than the last. It's as simple as that. It has nothing to do with the shapes themselves. (I told you IQ tests could be devious!) When you know what's happening, you can easily figure out that the next shape must have nine spaces filled in, so the answer must be:

Whatever type of question you're tackling, try approaching it from different angles until you crack it.

Ask yourself questions, explore your hunches, and try different possibilities. Be persistent, keep an open mind, and you might surprise yourself with how often you shout "Eureka!"

You said to approach problems from different angles!

Another Way to Test...........................

Research is being done into the link between IQ and reaction time. In one test, volunteers sit in front of an electronic panel. Bulbs light up at random, and the volunteers must move their hand as quickly as possible to push a button underneath the bulb. Their speed is measured and then compared with their results on written IQ tests.

From experiments like this, it seems that people with quick reactions are also quick at solving written puzzles. Try it yourself.

Become a Genius
REACT FAST!

WHAT YOU'LL NEED
* ✱ a ruler, preferably 12 inches (30 centimeters) long
* ✱ a friend

WHAT TO DO
1. Hold one arm straight out in front of you.
2. Ask your friend to hold the ruler by the top end while the 1-inch mark hangs between, but does not touch, your open thumb and first finger.
3. Have your friend let go of the ruler.
4. Catch the ruler between your fingers as quickly as possible, before it falls through and hits the floor.
5. When you catch the ruler, look to see where your fingers are. How many inches have gone through? Try it three times, record your best result, then let the rest of your friends try it. Who has the fastest reaction time? Perhaps one of you is a genius in the making!

CHAPTER SIX

BRAIN VERSUS COMPUTER

Can computers become geniuses? That's a question many top brains are working on right now.
Ever since the 1950s, the idea of artificial intelligence, or AI, has fascinated scientists. They have built computers that can do more and more complicated operations—but have they taught them to think?

One of the inventors of the computer, mathematics genius Alan Turing, came up with a way to test a computer's thinking ability.

The Turing Test

The rules of the Turing test are as follows:

 A computer is set up in one room, and a human judge sits in another.

 The judge "talks" to the computer by typing questions and answers on a keyboard.

 Sometimes another human takes control of the computer in the sealed room and has a conversation with the judge. At other times the computer itself communicates.

 The judge is never told whether he is talking to the computer or to another human.

 Another person records whether the judge can tell whether the computer or a human is talking.

To beat the Turing Test, a computer has to fool the judge into thinking that he is talking to an intelligent human being.

But isn't there more to it?

Sophisticated programs now allow computers to do extremely well in the Turing Test. For short periods of time, they can seem just like humans. There are still some things that confuse them, though, because conversations are much more complicated than you might imagine.

Think of two friends telling a joke, for example. How would you teach a computer that "Why did the chicken cross the road?" is funny?

This is one of the reasons why some scientists say computers will never become intelligent.

Human thought relies a great deal on feelings and emotions. Computers don't have emotions. For example, you could store your favorite book in a computer's memory, then make the computer do a search for a particular word. It would look like the computer was reading, but it would be very different from your experience reading the book. The computer wouldn't feel excited or scared or amused. It wouldn't know if the story was good or bad. It wouldn't have feelings about the information, so it would only appear to be intelligent.

Computers can do impressive things, but intelligent humans have to give them the instructions first. After all, when you listen to the radio, you don't think the stereo is intelligent, even though it seems to be performing amazing pieces of music!

Computers today are unbelievably fast and powerful, but the human brain is still the winner in most tests of thinking power.

Computers can churn through millions of operations every second, hour after hour, without getting tired or making a mistake. Our brains can't compete with that level of performance, but often we don't need to. We can decide where to focus our thoughts. We can find shortcuts, use our feelings, and go with our hunches. The human brain can also process many different kinds of information—sounds, colors, smells, and textures—and do a number of things at once.

In many challenging situations, only the brain has got what it takes to succeed. Genius thinking is much more than sheer processing power.

Checkmate ....

The Deep Blue computer program could look at 500 million chess moves every second. It was programmed with all the famous chess games and all the latest ideas. In 1996, World Chess Champion Garry Kasparov took on Deep Blue for a historic match.

It seems unbelievable, but Kasparov was favored to win—and he did. He led the computer into complicated situations in which its memory, power, and speed simply couldn't keep up. Only the human player could get a sense of the right moves and put together a winning plan.

In 1998, there was a rematch. Deep Blue—now called Deeper Blue—had been made even more powerful. It could look at one billion moves every second. This time the computer won. Kasparov put up a brave fight, but he eventually lost by a final score of 3 points to 2. His brain came close, though, even with all that brute electronic force up against him.

The next world chess champion may well be a computer program. It will still be a long time, however, before a computer can write a book about chess or decide on its own to play—or enjoy making the winning move.

How Computers Can Boost Your Brainpower

You can use your computer, or those in your school or local library, to boost your own chances of becoming a genius.

Great thinkers have always been willing to use the latest technology. Beethoven, for example, made use of the newly invented metronome to make sure his pieces were performed at exactly the right tempos. Never be afraid of new gadgets. They don't replace human brainpower, but they allow you to keep your energy for the most important kinds of thinking.

For example, if you were planning a new look for your bedroom, you could use a calculator to check the measurements and calculations. This would save your brainpower for dreaming up new design ideas.

If you play chess, checkers, backgammon, or bridge, use computers to give you the ultimate challenge. It's a great way to learn and improve, because you can keep increasing the skill level and pushing yourself to play better. When the computer wins, try to see how it happened. Learn from your own mistakes. Trust your judgment, and keep challenging even the most powerful machines.

Use the Internet to build up your knowledge and explore the areas that interest you. Geniuses communicate with other experts, so you can send e-mail and chat online to swap ideas and gain inspiration from others.

You can even spend some of your time playing computer games to improve your reflexes and problem-solving ability. Try the reaction-time experiment on page 57 before and after playing a computer game for 15 minutes, to see whether your reflexes have improved.

CHAPTER SEVEN

GENIUS CHARACTERS

Even the most powerful computer in the world can't be a genius, because it has no character. It can remember and calculate quickly and accurately and handle huge amounts of information—but it can't think about the information the same way we can. It has no feelings, no opinions, and no moments of madness.

Investigate the great human geniuses and you'll see that they all have special aspects of their character, qualities that allowed them to go beyond what's already been achieved. Their lives hold many of the secrets of putting great ideas into practice. Learn from their examples to boost your own chances of becoming a genius.

Have Fun

Leonardo da Vinci was well known for his jokes and funny stories. Galileo had a busy social life and was also a great jokester. Bill Gates, the genius behind software giant Microsoft, has been described as a "perpetual teenager." He has said that one of his favorite hobbies was playing with earth-moving equipment on building sites.

Be Inquisitive

Geniuses spend their lives asking questions about the world around them.

Leonardo da Vinci filled many notebooks with his explorations. Here's a snippet:

> I roamed the countryside searching for answers to things I did not understand. Why shells existed on the tops of mountains... why the thunder lasts a longer time than that which causes it... how the various circles of water form around the spot which has been struck by a stone... why a bird sustains itself in the air...

The typical genius questions are "why?" and "how?"

Be Brave

Geniuses simply aren't afraid of making mistakes. Orville and Wilbur Wright crashed several times and ruined many airplanes before they finally got off the ground. Thomas Edison failed thousands of times before he managed to turn electricity into light. He told his friends that, because he knew so many ways that didn't work, he was much closer than any other inventor to finding the right answer.

Geniuses must also be prepared to make waves and face opposition in society. New ideas can seem strange and even frightening to others, and great thinkers are often described as disruptive and rebellious. For example, some people are still angry about Charles Darwin's theory of evolution, because his ideas conflict with religious teachings—and we've had more than a century to recover!

Keep Trying ....

Thomas Edison once said that genius was "1 percent inspiration and 99 percent perspiration."

To become a genius, you must be prepared to work long and hard, often in the face of great obstacles.

Be Inspired.....................................

The answers you're looking for might be close by—
you just have to know where to look.

Leonardo da Vinci wandered through the countryside
looking at nature, and many other great thinkers have
found their inspiration outside, too. Travel is another
good source of inspiration. Mozart picked up many
good musical ideas during his travels. While still in his
teens, Albert Einstein persuaded his parents to let him
tour the large cities of Italy. He came back with some
exciting ideas.

Tips to help you be inspired:

 Spend time in nature, looking at the way
animals and plants behave.

 Take every opportunity you get to travel, both in
this country and abroad.

 Start a scrapbook and fill it with photographs,
leaves, newspaper cuttings, tickets—everything
that reminds you of your most interesting
experiences.

Stay Fit......................................

There's an ancient saying, *mens sana in corpore sano,* which means "a healthy mind in a healthy body." It's very important for you to feel good and for your body to be operating at its best, so that your mind can also function powerfully.

As well as being a genius philosopher, poet, and statesman, Sophocles was a champion athlete who won many trophies.

Top mathematician Ronald Graham is an expert trampolinist, bowler, and tennis player. Leonardo da Vinci was famous for his strength, agility, and ability as a horseman. Inventor World Chess Champion Garry Kasparov spends as much time training his body—running, swimming, and lifting weights—as he does his incredible brain.

Tips for Keeping Fit

Aerobic exercise: Your brain makes up only 2 percent of your body weight, but it uses an amazing 20 percent of the oxygen you breathe in. It's crucial that your brain be supplied with plenty of oxygen. Swimming, fast walking, running, soccer, tennis, and other sports improve what's called your aerobic fitness—your ability to take in oxygen. Exercise can double your aerobic fitness.

Strength: Garry Kasparov has said that the stronger he feels, the stronger he thinks. Boosting your physical strength makes you feel more positive and improves your persistence and stamina. Under careful supervision, you can use weights or practice field sports like the javelin and discus to improve your strength. Leonardo da Vinci was said to be able to bend horseshoes with his bare hands!

Flexibility: Da Vinci was described as graceful and poised. He had studied the way the human body works, and he made sure that his worked without strain. If you've ever pulled a muscle or strained some part of your body, you know how much mental energy this takes away. To have free, creative thoughts it's important to feel limber and relaxed.

Before sitting down to work or think, spend a few minutes loosening up. Slowly roll your head clockwise and counterclockwise. Shake your arms and legs. Carefully bend down to touch your toes, then stretch your arms up toward the ceiling. Do this a few times before you get started, and again every so often while you're hard at work.

Balance: Gymnastics, rollerblading, and skateboarding are all excellent ways of improving your balance. Check your balance now by standing on one leg. How long can you stand like that without falling over? Da Vinci's body was under his control just as completely as his mind.

Diet: Your diet must also be properly balanced. Make sure you supply your brain with all the nutrients it needs to work well. Eat a diet low in fats and sugar and rich in fresh fruits and vegetables, and drink plenty of water. Never eat so much that you feel full and tired, but be sure to keep up your energy levels throughout the day. Savor the food you eat—how it looks and smells as well as tastes—and make every mealtime an inspiring, relaxing, refueling event.

Become a Genius
HEALTHY MIND/HEALTHY BODY

Before you next do some exercise, spend a few
minutes taking the following test. The answers are on page 73.
Keep a note of your score and how long you took.

THE BEFORE TEST
1. 26 + 17 = ?
2. 42 − 9 = ?
3. 7 x 4 = ?
4. What number comes next? 3 10 17 24 _
5. Which is the odd one out? car, elephant, bicycle, table, cat
6. Which word is the opposite of warm?
              hot, shiver, like, cool, south
7. Which letter comes next? c f i l _

Now, go and do some exercise for at least half an hour. When
you've finished, as soon as you've got your breath back, take
this second test. The answers are on page 73. How well did
you do this time? Compare your score and your speed. It's
likely that you did even better, thanks to the extra oxygen
being pumped to your brain.

THE AFTER TEST
1. 16 + 8 = ?
2. 30 − 7 = ?
3. 5 x 9 = ?
4. Which number comes next? 20 15 10 5 _
5. Which two of these words mean the same?
              walk, rest, freeze, relax, take
6. What is the opposite of give? lose, work, take, in, present
7. Which letter comes next in this sequence? r q p o _

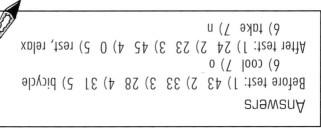

Don't Worry ....

You're wrong if you think geniuses are all perfect, well-rounded individuals who are good at everything. Many had to contend with major problems. Geniuses are just very good at overcoming obstacles. Think of it this way: a genius is not someone who is perfect, but someone who constantly strives to make the world—and him or herself—better.

Physicist Stephen Hawking is virtually paralyzed, moves around in a wheelchair, and speaks only with the help of a computer. He wrote one of the most successful books ever and continues to lead the world to new levels of understanding. Edison and Beethoven both lost their hearing, and Alexander the Great and Julius Caesar both suffered epileptic fits—yet they all achieved greatness.

Math genius Paul Erdos was extremely absent-minded and messy. Archimedes was said to be so forgetful that he often missed meals. When super-intelligent people have something important on their minds, they are often unaware of their surroundings.

Einstein had a particularly disorganized mind and a chaotic workroom. Nobody was allowed to dust or clean up, and it looked like a complete mess—that is, to everyone except Einstein, who insisted he knew where everything was. In his daily life, however, he was often very forgetful.

As we've already seen, Einstein was also bad at math. In fact, many of the great geniuses failed at particular subjects. It's not surprising that many great thinkers were dismissed as failures by their teachers. Charles Darwin got very bad reports at school, but went on to discover amazing things about life on Earth.

No matter how many obstacles they have to get around, truly great geniuses will always make it. It's in their character to succeed.

CHAPTER EIGHT

GENIUS THINKING

You have an incredible brain. To be a genius, you need to start using it like a genius.

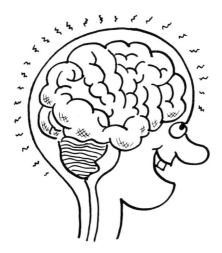

Your brain weighs about 3 pounds (1.4 kilograms) and contains about 100 billion nerve cells. It can perform millions of operations every second.

After he died in 1955, Albert Einstein's brain was removed and preserved in a laboratory. Scientists were curious to see whether it was particularly large or unusually formed in some way. What scientists discovered was that Einstein had a perfectly normal brain, but he used it in a particular way.

Einstein had formed many more connections between brain cells than other people. His thinking methods were very good for linking things together, learning from everything, and coming up with new solutions and exciting ideas. Einstein used an unusually large portion of his brain, which made him an excellent "whole-brain" thinker.

Your Two Brains ....

Did you know that you really have two brains—a left brain and a right brain? Geniuses use both sides together, and you can learn to do that too.

In the 1960s, a scientist named Roger Sperry discovered that there are two distinct sides of the brain. He found that each side has a particular set of functions.

The left side is where the brain mostly handles

* words
* numbers
* lists
* decisions
* plans

The right side tends to deal with

* colors
* ideas
* shapes
* dreams
* imagination

Sperry discovered that the most intelligent and successful people were good at using both sides of their brain at the same time.

Children tend to be very "right-brained." They think in pictures and stories and enjoy playing and experimenting with their imagination.

Adults, on the other hand, are usually much more "left-brained" and logical. They make lists, count things, and make decisions.

Geniuses tend to be somewhere in between. The more of your brain that you can use at any one time, the more powerful your thinking will be.

Some Whole-Brain Thinkers

Leonardo da Vinci planned his paintings very carefully. He made detailed notes about his colors and worked out the measurements and proportions with great care. His notebooks are full of intricate sketches and notes. ➤

Painting takes more right-brain thinking (colors, shapes, spaces, imagination), but planning and preparation is more left-brain (numbers, measurements, decisions, facts). Da Vinci was using both sides of his brain at once, creating amazing pictures like the *Mona Lisa*.

Da Vinci was also a great inventor. Again, you can look in his notebooks to find drawings of tanks, aircraft, diving equipment, and so on. What you notice most is the artistic way in which he sketched them. His work is covered with doodles and scribbles, people, animals, and patterns. Once again, he was doing right-brain thinking (pictures, ideas, doodles) and left-brain thinking (plans, details, numbers) at the same time. No wonder he came up with so many incredible inventions!

Scientists Isaac Newton and Thomas Edison both used artistic sketches and doodles to help them think. Beethoven's manuscripts include drawings and scribbled ideas among his notes. Painter Pablo Picasso made some very detailed mechanical drawings as well as wildly imaginative masterpieces.

Excellent work, Picasso. If you keep this up, you'll make a fine engineer one day.

Albert Einstein used his imagination to help him with his scientific investigations. He once pictured himself riding on a beam of light holding a clock, to help him figure out the connection between speed and time. He was an expert in switching on the logical and the imaginative sides of his brain at once.

Become a Whole-Brain Thinker..............

Use your right brain. Make your written work as imaginative as possible. Use different colors whenever you can. Sketch out your ideas in doodles, patterns, and pictures. At the same time, use your left brain. Keep your work organized, and pay attention to details. Make lists, draw diagrams, and label everything carefully.

To help you solve tricky problems, use your imagination. Picture yourself inside the problem, as if it were a dream. Let your mind wander to amazing new places, and you might be surprised at the answers you come up with. Perhaps singing at the same time helps, or drawing a cartoon to represent your ideas.

Feel free to doodle, make a model, or play a musical instrument. Activate your right brain to help with problem-solving—don't leave it all to your logical left side.

When you want to come up with ideas for stories, plays, pictures, or poems, bring your left brain in to help. Make clear lists of all the ideas you have, then give them all marks (1–10) for brilliance. Draw diagrams, make calculations, and do some careful planning. Using your left brain in this way gives you extra thinking power.

Become a Genius
BOOST YOUR MEMORY

WHAT YOU'LL NEED
✱ a pen ✱ some paper

WHAT TO DO
1. Read this shopping list through for one minute:

bananas	jam
milk	bread
sausages	trash bags
chocolate	sprouts
tissues	candy

Many great geniuses have had incredible memories. They learned a large number of facts and figures and kept up to date with the latest ideas.

The trick is to organize information into lists (left brain), then use your imagination to turn the lists into stories (right brain).

2. Cover up the list and write down as many of the things on the list as you can remember.
3. Uncover the list.

How did you do?

One way to learn the list would be to use your imagination and turn it into a strange story:

Imagine peeling a banana and finding that inside the skin there was nothing but milk, which runs down your hands. The milk pours out across the floor, and you notice that there are sausages floating in it!

The river of milk makes a waterfall, and the sausages drop down into a pool of thick, runny chocolate. The chocolate splashes into your face, and you have to wipe it away with a tissue. But the tissues are covered with jam, and you end up in an even stickier mess than before! The only other thing nearby is a slice of bread. Imagine how the bread feels against your face. You toss the bread away into a trash bag, but it bounces out, because the bag is full of moldy sprouts. They smell terrible! You lift one out and it transforms into a piece of candy, which you pop into your mouth.

Spend a couple of minutes going back through this story. Picture it all happening to you. Imagine the sights, sounds, smells, tastes, and textures of this weird tale. Now, can you remember the ten items on the shopping list? The story started with peeling a banana.

You can use this trick with anything you need to remember. Simply make a list of words, then write a little story in your mind to link them all together. With practice you can remember hundreds of things!

Some Other Good Memory Tips ············

Be observant and alert. You won't remember things unless you've seen or heard them in the first place.

If you can't remember a word or name, run through the alphabet in your mind. Ask yourself whether it begins with *a, b,* or *c*... and so on, until you jog your memory.

What do you look like when you're straining to remember? Do you have any habits, like scratching your head, rubbing your chin, or folding your arms? If you do, then make sure you always do these things when you need to remember something quickly.

Smells are very useful for bringing back memories. If you forget something, try to remember what you could smell when you last saw or heard it. For example, if you were washing your face when you had a good idea, but you've forgotten the idea, you could sniff a bar of soap to help jog your brain.

Leave yourself reminders. Write on your hand, tie a knot in the corner of your handkerchief, or ask other people to remind you. Always be on the lookout for easy ways to remember things.

Creative Thinking ....

Start using your memory in creative ways, and you'll give your imagination an excellent workout. Imagination is vital to thinking like a genius. Geniuses rely on their imaginations to have amazing creative thoughts.

Look at this picture.
What do you think it is?

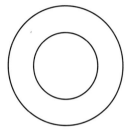

Most people reply to this question with a single answer, but there are many possible answers. It could be an eye, a fried egg, a wheel, a doorknob, a cowboy hat from above, a doughnut, a rubber ring—there's no end to the possibilities.

I'm sure you could come up with more ideas—just as soon as you see that there's no right (or wrong) answer. All you have to do is use your imagination.

Never Assume Anything ....

Always keep an open mind. Scientific geniuses like Isaac Newton and Stephen Hawking have always looked for fresh ideas. They were brave enough to challenge the experts who came before them, and to see what they could discover for themselves. Other people might have found answers, but they're not necessarily the only answers.

Become a Genius
FIND NEW WAYS OF
DOING THINGS (1)

WHAT YOU'LL NEED
∗ a book or magazine

WHAT TO DO
Pick three sentences from your book or magazine. Your challenge is to rewrite each sentence so that the new version means exactly the same as the original. The only rule is that you can't use any of the original words. You need to think of new ways to say the same things. It doesn't matter if the new version sounds a bit complicated. It's all excellent practice in seeing new possibilities. For example, if one of the lines reads:

"The two boys left home at 8:45 and boarded the bus for school."

... you might re-write it as:

"A couple of young males departed their house when clocks read a quarter to nine, then were driven in a yellow vehicle toward their place of learning."

An individual little pace for one guy, a single massive bound for everyone.

Reverse Things ....

Many great ideas have come when people imagined things backward, or thought about opposites. For example, how do you make a busy intersection safer? One local council thought in reverse, and made the junction even busier by letting the traffic approach from every direction. This slowed down the traffic and made everyone take greater care at the intersection— and there were fewer accidents!

Become a Genius
FIND NEW WAYS OF DOING THINGS (2)

WHAT TO DO

Come up with as many answers as you can for the following questions:

- How could you break an egg?
- What could you use to waste water in your home?
- How could you make your school as boring as possible?

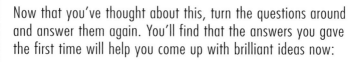

Now that you've thought about this, turn the questions around and answer them again. You'll find that the answers you gave the first time will help you come up with brilliant ideas now:

- Design a device for preventing eggs from getting broken.
- How could you conserve water at home?
- What could you do to make your school more exciting?

Take Another Look ....

Geniuses need to be able to see problems from different angles. Your first attempt to crack a puzzle might not be the best way.

Become a Genius
FIND NEW WAYS OF DOING THINGS (3)

WHAT TO DO

1. See how quickly you can count the number of colored squares in box A:

A

2. Now do the same with box B:

B

WHAT HAPPENED?

How did you approach this task? Simply counting the colored squares in box A is probably the quickest and easiest thing to do. But with box B, the best approach is to count the white squares. There are 5 white squares in a box of 25 squares, so there have to be 20 colored squares.

There are often very quick ways of solving problems. Try approaching them from different angles.

Boost Your Senses ....

Leonardo da Vinci once said that that the average person looks without seeing, listens without hearing, touches without feeling, eats without tasting, and inhales without smelling. Da Vinci had amazing senses, which he used to explore the world and seek inspiration.

The better your senses, the more likely you are to become a genius. Spend time practicing the arts of seeing, hearing, touching, smelling, and tasting.

Become a Genius
BOOST YOUR SENSES

SIGHT

1. Spend 10 seconds focusing on something in the far distance, then switch to looking at something nearby. Repeat this change of focus five times. Next, sit by a window and see what you can see. Spend 10 minutes picking out as many different colors outside as you can.

2. Rub your hands together for about 15 seconds, then cup your palms over your closed eyes. Relax in this position for 2 minutes, then take your hands away—but keep your eyes closed. Now slowly open your eyes. The world will seem brighter, the colors sharper. Practice this technique at the start and end of every day to keep your eyesight strong and clear.

Leave me alone. I'm boosting my senses!

HEARING

1. What can you hear at this moment? Spend 2 minutes noting every different sound you can pick up.
2. Experiment by listening to different types of music while you're working. Which music helps your thinking most? On the other hand, is silence what you prefer?

TOUCH

1. Practice your touch skills with a friend. Close your eyes while your friend places different objects in your hand. Can you guess what each one is? Change places so that you can challenge your friend, and try to come up with unusual textures.

2. Choose five different textures, and try to describe them in as many different ways as possible. Use the most descriptive words you can think of.

SMELL

1. Close your eyes and try to imagine the following smells: bacon frying, chocolate, newly cut grass, cheese, an animal.
2. How many different smells can you pick up in the room where you're sitting now? It might help to wander around.

TASTE

1. The next time you eat a meal, see how many different flavors you can pick out. Can you identify any of the individual ingredients?
2. Imagine these tastes as vividly as you can: orange juice, potato chips, celery, cake, tomato sauce.

CHAPTER NINE

THE GENIUS CHALLENGE

After reading about some of the greatest thinkers and learning plenty of their secrets, how close are you to becoming a genius? The Genius Challenge will tell you.

You have half an hour to complete the following questions. Before you start, spend a few moments relaxing your mind. Make sure you're feeling alert and positive. Work with paper and a pen. Prepare to use all the skills you've learned to think clearly and creatively. Figure out what each question is asking you, and think of the best way to respond. You can play music, walk around, juggle, or do anything you like to help your thought process.

Use your whole brain, and think like a genius.

Become a Genius
GENIUS CHALLENGE

1. Observation

a) How many edges does a penny have?

b) Which of these is the right shape for a Yield sign on the road?

A   B   C   D

c) What's wrong with this picture?

2. Words

a) Which two words in this list mean the same?

loud dull boring hitting sorry

b) Which word is the odd one out?

loop part shell long keep

c) Which word comes after "garage" and before "opener"?

3. Numbers

a) Which number is the odd one out?

621 245 711 342

b) Which number comes next?

1 2 4 7 11

c) If 5389 becomes 8953, then 4067 becomes _. ➤

4. Shapes

Which shape comes next in this sequence?

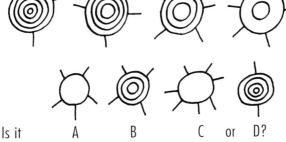

Is it   A   B   C or D?

5. Memory

Spend a few minutes learning these words, then cover the page and write down as many of them as you can remember:

book, water, watch, baby, CD, hammer, car, elephant, cake, sun

6. Logic

Ben has only two pets. One of his pets is a dog. Charlotte has a cat named Blackie. Blackie loves sardines.

From those details only, which of the following facts is definitely true?

a)   Ben doesn't have a cat.   c)   Charlotte's cat is black.

b)   Charlotte has a dog.   d)   Charlotte's cat will eat fish.

7. Creativity

a)   What could this be?
Think of as many different answers as you can.

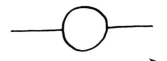

➤

b) How could you keep your school free from litter? How many ideas can you come up with?

c) How could you keep your bedroom safe from burglars? Write down all the ideas you come up with.

Now, what was that number again?

8. Puzzles

a) Two Australians are standing on a beach. One is tall and the other is short. The short Australian is the tall Australian's son, but the tall Australian is not the short Australian's father. How can that be possible?

b) Which is heavier: a pound of iron or a pound of feathers?

c) What has a bottom at the top?

Genius Scores ....

How far along the road to genius have you come?

0–20 points:

You have a lot of work to do, but you can improve dramatically if you follow the examples set by the geniuses in this book. Read the book again and make sure you try all the experiments and tests. Try to have fun boosting your brainpower, and don't be discouraged: your journey to genius is only just beginning.

21–40 points:

You've made a good start, but you'll need to master more skills before you can come closer to genius. Set yourself targets to improve, and try to find other books about thinking and brainpower. You've proved you've got what it takes, so make sure you go all the way!

41–60 points:

This is a very good score, and it shows that you are already thinking like a genius. Make a note of the questions where you lost points, and give those areas a little more attention. Be proud of your amazing brain, and keep up the good work.

61–80 points: Excellent work. With a little more practice, you're going to achieve some incredible things. Spend a little time improving your thinking zone, and perhaps learn to juggle to release your imagination. You've learned a great deal from this book. Now is your chance to start putting it all into practice.

More than 80 points:

Congratulations! You are doing everything right, and there's no reason why you can't become a well-known genius. You need to decide where to concentrate your brainpower, but make sure to explore a variety of interests to keep you inspired. Find other people who think like geniuses, and swap tips and ideas. Keep practicing all the techniques explained in this book, and never miss an opportunity for learning.

THE GENIUS RACES